D1614298

GRACE

Ships

by Thomas K. Adamson

BELLWETHER MEDIA · MINNEAPOLIS, MN

BLASTOFF!
2
READERS

Note to Librarians, Teachers, and Parents:

Blastoff! Readers are carefully developed by literacy experts and combine standards-based content with developmentally appropriate text.

Level 1 provides the most support through repetition of high-frequency words, light text, predictable sentence patterns, and strong visual support.

Level 2 offers early readers a bit more challenge through varied simple sentences, increased text load, and less repetition of high-frequency words.

Level 3 advances early-fluent readers toward fluency through increased text and concept load, less reliance on visuals, longer sentences, and more literary language.

Level 4 builds reading stamina by providing more text per page, increased use of punctuation, greater variation in sentence patterns, and increasingly challenging vocabulary.

Level 5 encourages children to move from "learning to read" to "reading to learn" by providing even more text, varied writing styles, and less familiar topics.

Whichever book is right for your reader, Blastoff! Readers are the perfect books to build confidence and encourage a love of reading that will last a lifetime!

This edition first published in 2017 by Bellwether Media, Inc.

No part of this publication may be reproduced in whole or in part without written permission of the publisher. For information regarding permission, write to Bellwether Media, Inc., Attention: Permissions Department, 5357 Penn Avenue South, Minneapolis, MN 55419.

Library of Congress Cataloging-in-Publication Data

Names: Adamson, Thomas K., 1970- author.
Title: Ships / by Thomas K. Adamson.
Description: Minneapolis, MN : Bellwether Media, Inc., 2017. | Series: Blastoff! Readers. Mighty Machines in Action | Audience: Ages 5-8. | Audience: K to grade 3. | Includes bibliographical references and index.
Identifiers: LCCN 2016036733 (print) | LCCN 2016038097 (ebook) | ISBN 9781626176089 (hardcover : alk. paper) | ISBN 9781681033389 (ebook)
Subjects: LCSH: Ships–Juvenile literature.
Classification: LCC VM150 .A38 2017 (print) | LCC VM150 (ebook) | DDC 623.82–dc23
LC record available at https://lccn.loc.gov/2016036733

Editor: Christina Leighton   Designer: Steve Porter

Printed in the United States of America, North Mankato, MN.

Table of Contents

ARRIVING AT PORT

A large ship cuts through the water. It carries a big load of **cargo**.

cargo

The ship took weeks to cross the ocean!

The ship needs a lot of room to turn. A tugboat guides it into the **port**.

tugboat

Then the ship blows its horn.
It has arrived!

SHIPS IN ACTION

Ships travel all around the world. They carry people and cargo across large bodies of water.

8

Ships come in many different types and sizes.

THE LARGEST CONTAINER SHIP

MSC Oscar

height: 240 feet (73 meters)

holds up to 19,224 containers

average school bus

width: 194 feet (59 meters)

Cruise ships bring passengers to places.

MACHINE PROFILE
CARNIVAL VICTORY CRUISE SHIP

- **Pools:** 4
- **Mini golf course:** 1
- **Guests:** up to 2,754

Supertankers carry huge amounts of oil. Cargo ships hold thousands of **containers** with goods inside.

DECKS, HULLS, AND PROPELLERS

Ships have one or more **decks**. Military **aircraft carriers** have giant, flat decks.

deck

fighter jet

These are big enough for **fighter jets** to land on!

Most ships are made of steel. A ship usually has a rounded **hull** that helps it float.

hull

propellers

A large engine and **propellers** in back make the ship move. A **rudder** steers it.

The front of a ship is the **bow**.
It cuts through water.

bow

stern

The back of a ship is the **stern**. At the very bottom of a ship is the **keel**.

radar

Captains control ships. Computers track the ships' locations.

Ships also use **radar** for location. This finds the distance to land and other ships.

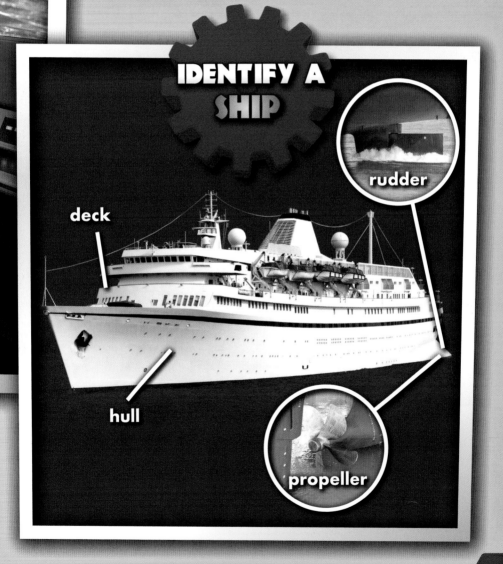

IDENTIFY A SHIP

deck

hull

rudder

propeller

Ships carry heavy loads across thousands of miles.

These huge machines sail
oceans far and wide!

Glossary

aircraft carriers—military ships that carry airplanes

bow—the front of the ship

cargo—something that is carried by a ship

containers—large boxes that hold goods

decks—flat parts on the tops of ships

fighter jets—military planes used in battle

hull—the main body of a ship

keel—the very bottom of a ship

port—a place where ships load and unload

propellers—sets of spinning blades

radar—a device that finds the location and distance of something

rudder—the part of the ship that steers

stern—the back of the ship

supertankers—large ships that carry oil

To Learn More

AT THE LIBRARY

Allen, Kenny. *Aircraft Carriers.* New York, N.Y.: Gareth Stevens Pub., 2013.

Bowman, Chris. *Monster Ships.* Minneapolis, Minn.: Bellwether Media, 2014.

Meister, Cari. *Ships.* Minneapolis, Minn.: Jump!, 2014.

ON THE WEB

Learning more about ships is as easy as 1, 2, 3.

1. Go to www.factsurfer.com.

2. Enter "ships" into the search box.

3. Click the "Surf" button and you will see a list of related web sites.

With factsurfer.com, finding more information is just a click away.

Index

The images in this book are reproduced through the courtesy of: Ruth Peterkin, front cover; Alex Kolokythas Photography, pp. 4, 4-5; Sheila Fitzgerald, pp. 6-7; Isantilli, pp. 8-9; VectorPlotnikoff, p. 9 (school bus); NAN728, pp. 10, 20-21; Shi Yali, pp. 10-11; michaelbwatkins, pp. 12-13; US Navy Photo/ Alamy, p. 13; Nightman1965, pp. 14, 14-15, 17; Alan Smillie, pp. 16-17, 19; Cultura Limited/ SuperStock, pp. 18-19; EdwinPics, p. 19 (rudder); Hazlan Abdul Hakim, p. 19 (propeller).